mighty machines
SHIPS
& SUBMARINES

Written by
Chris Oxlade

Illustrated by
Mike Taylor

p

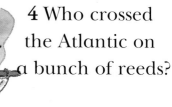

This is a Parragon Publishing Book
First published in 2001

Parragon Publishing
Queen Street House
4 Queen Street
Bath BA1 1HE, UK

Copyright © Parragon 2001

Produced by

David West 𝕏 Children's Books
7 Princeton Court
55 Felsham Road
Putney
London SW15 1AZ, UK

British Library Cataloguing-in-Publication Data

A catalogue record for this book is available from
the British Library.

ISBN 0-75254-692-9

Printed in U.A.E

Designers
David West
Aarti Parmar
Illustrator
Mike Taylor
(SGA)
Cartoonist
Peter Wilks
(SGA)
Editor
James Pickering
Consultant
Steve Parker

CONTENTS

? Who crossed the Atlantic on a bunch of reeds?

In 1970, Thor Heyerdahl, a Norwegian scientist and explorer, and his seven crew, crossed the Atlantic Ocean in a sailing boat made from reeds. The trip showed that sailors from Ancient Egypt could have made the journey in reed boats thousands of years before Christopher Columbus in 1492.

Papyrus reed boat Ra II

Is it true?
Dug-out canoes are still used today.

Yes. Dug-outs are still made and used in many parts of the world. They are used for fishing and paddling along rivers. Fishermen who live on islands in the Pacific, such as Tonga, sail out to sea in dug-out canoes with outriggers (small side hulls) which help the canoe to balance.

? Who hollowed out logs?

Ancient people made boats called dug-out canoes by hollowing out large tree trunks. They scraped and chipped the wood out with simple tools. Dug-out canoes were amongst the first types of boat.

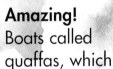

Amazing!

Boats called quaffas, which were sailed on the Euphrates River in Syria and Iraq, were made like baskets. In fact, the word quaffa means basket. The boats were made of branches woven together and covered in tar. Large quaffas could carry 20 passengers.

5

Dug-out canoe

? Who went fishing in animal skins?

Fishermen in Wales and Ireland used to go fishing in small boats called coracles or curraghs. They were made by covering a framework of bendy sticks with animal skins. A few fishermen still use canvas coracles today.

Coracle

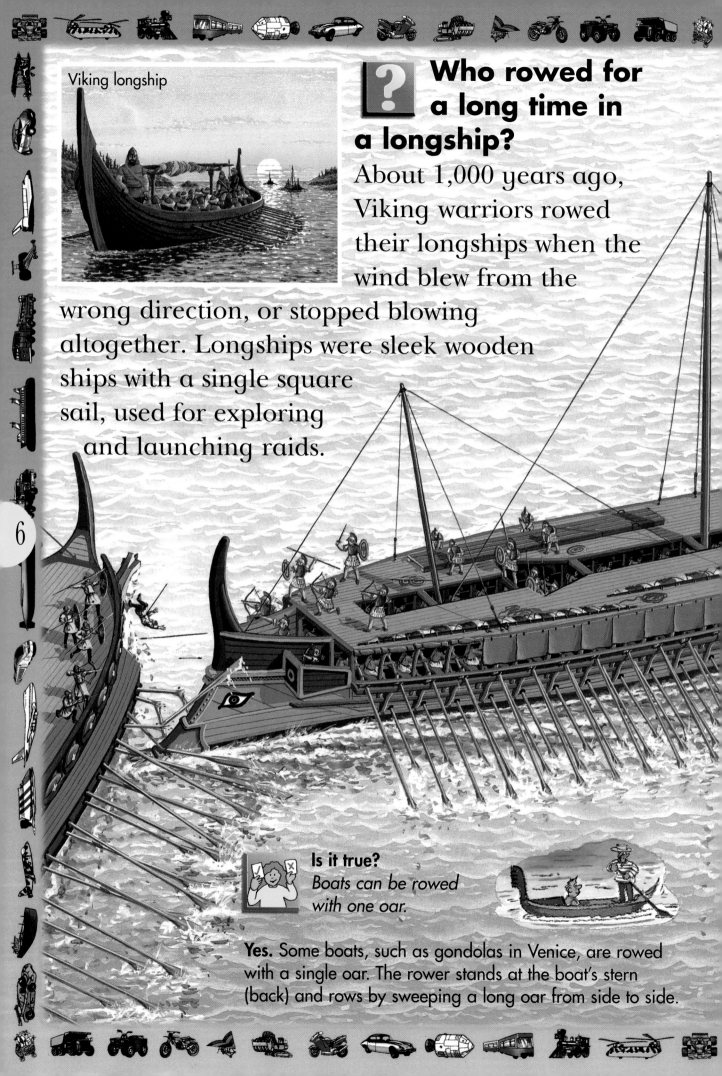

Viking longship

Who rowed for a long time in a longship?

About 1,000 years ago, Viking warriors rowed their longships when the wind blew from the wrong direction, or stopped blowing altogether. Longships were sleek wooden ships with a single square sail, used for exploring and launching raids.

Is it true?
Boats can be rowed with one oar.

Yes. Some boats, such as gondolas in Venice, are rowed with a single oar. The rower stands at the boat's stern (back) and rows by sweeping a long oar from side to side.

Who rowed in battle?

The Ancient Greeks fought in warships called galleys that they rowed into battle. Slaves did the rowing while soldiers fought on deck. Galleys had a sharp ram at the bow (front) to sink enemy ships. A galley with three banks of oars on each side was called a trireme.

Amazing!
Many people have rowed across the Atlantic Ocean or Pacific Ocean. And some have done it solo (on their own). The journey across the Atlantic takes two months or more, and across the Pacific four months or more.

Ancient Greek trireme

Rowing eights

Who steers an eight?

An "eight" is the crew of a racing rowing boat. The ninth member, the cox, tells the rowers what pace to row at, and steers with a small rudder at the back of the boat.

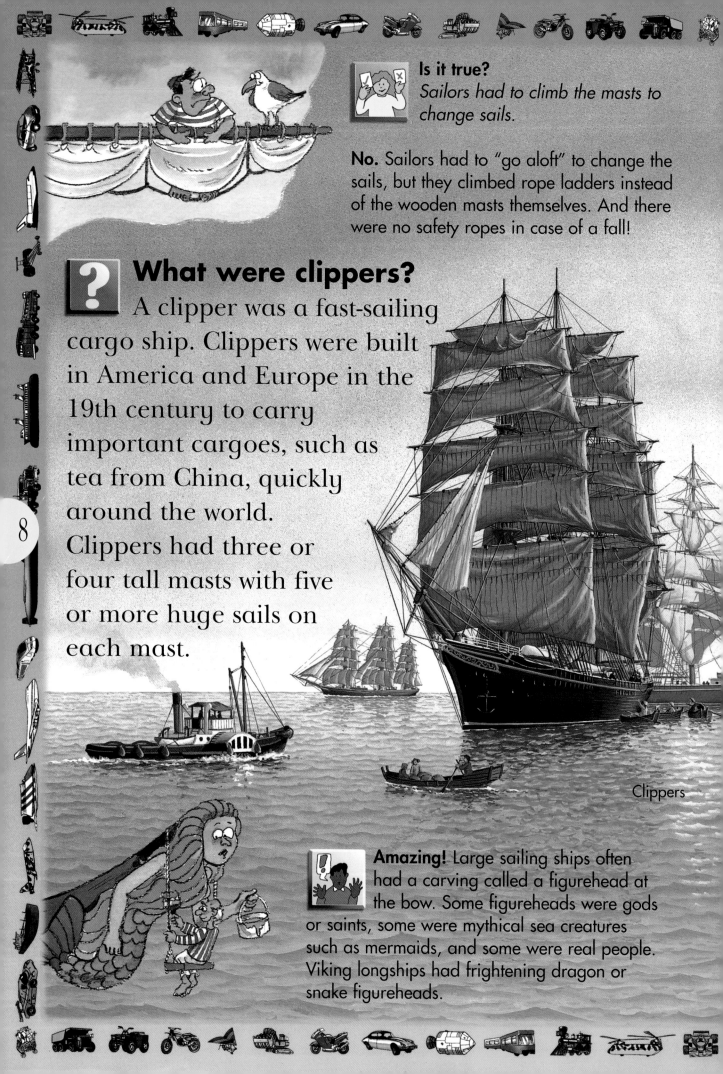

Is it true?
Sailors had to climb the masts to change sails.

No. Sailors had to "go aloft" to change the sails, but they climbed rope ladders instead of the wooden masts themselves. And there were no safety ropes in case of a fall!

? What were clippers?

A clipper was a fast-sailing cargo ship. Clippers were built in America and Europe in the 19th century to carry important cargoes, such as tea from China, quickly around the world. Clippers had three or four tall masts with five or more huge sails on each mast.

Clippers

Amazing! Large sailing ships often had a carving called a figurehead at the bow. Some figureheads were gods or saints, some were mythical sea creatures such as mermaids, and some were real people. Viking longships had frightening dragon or snake figureheads.

What was a galleon?

Galleons were trading and fighting ships used in the 15th and 16th centuries. The galleon *Mayflower* took the first pilgrims to America in 1620.

Mayflower

Who went to sea on a junk?

Chinese sailors have been going to sea in ships called junks for more than a thousand years. Junks have cloth sails strengthened with bamboo poles. Large junks have five masts. Junks were the first ships to have a rudder to help them steer.

Chinese junk

? Who sailed under the skull and crossbones?

The skull and crossbones was the flag of pirates, who flew it from their ships. Pirates attacked ships especially in the Mediterranean and Caribbean. They often killed the crew, stole the cargo and sometimes the ship itself!

Amazing! The famous pirate Blackbeard set off firecrackers in his huge beard to frighten people. Blackbeard's buried treasure has never been found.

? What was a Corsair's galley?

Corsairs were pirates in the Mediterranean about 400 years ago. They sailed in galleys, rowed by slaves chained to their oars.

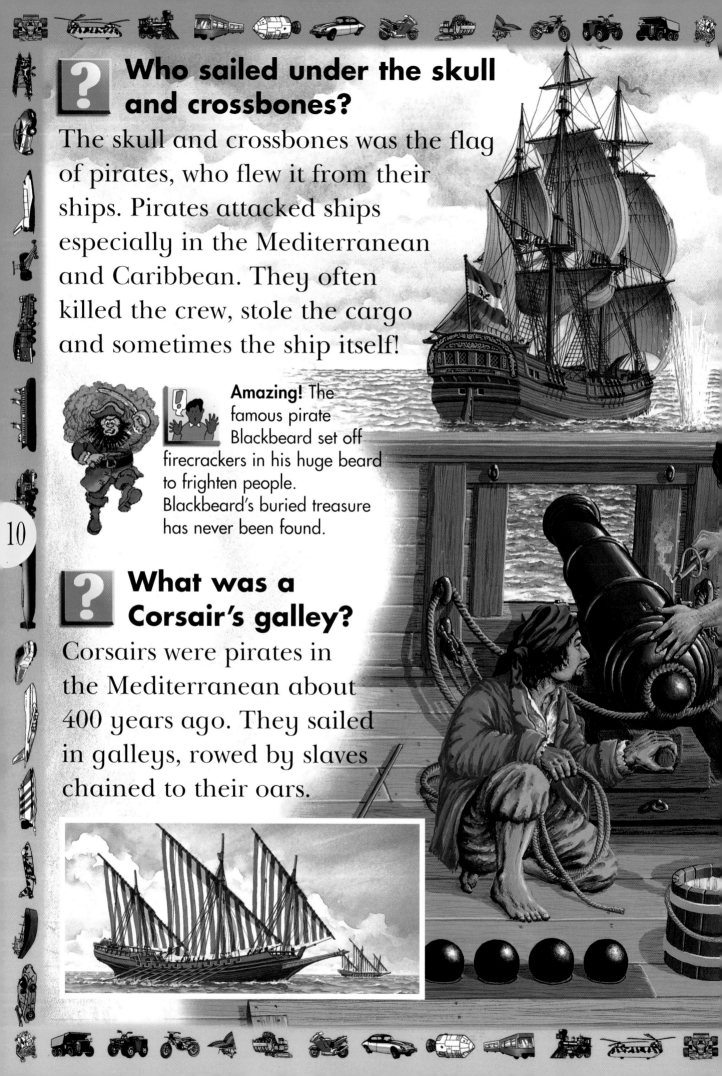

Skull and crossbones

Is it true?
Sailors slept in beds.

No. Ordinary sailors slept in hammocks which hung from the deck above. Only the captain and officers had proper beds in their cabins.

Bonny and Read

11

? Who were Bonny and Read?

Mary Read and Anne Bonny were a famous pirate team. Read ran away to sea disguised as a boy and Bonny joined a pirate ship aged 16. They met when Bonny's ship captured Read's.

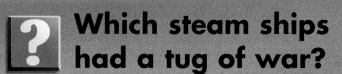

? Which steam ships had a tug of war?

In 1845, two British naval steamships had a tug of war, to see if propellers were better than paddles for making a ship move through the water. HMS *Rattler*, with a propeller, pulled HMS *Alecto*, which had paddles, backwards at nearly three knots.

HMS Rattler

Is it true?
A ship's speed is measured in knots.

Yes. One knot is equal to 1.15 mph. Sailors used to measure speed by dropping a log tied to a rope overboard and counting how quickly the knots tied in the rope went by.

12

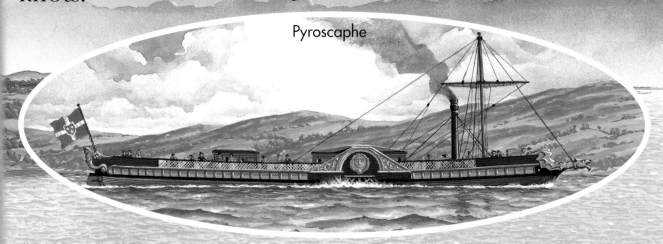

Pyroscaphe

? What was the first steam boat?

The first boat to be propelled by a steam engine was called *Pyroscaphe*. It was built in France by Jouffroy d'Abbans, and had two paddle wheels. In 1783 it worked for just 15 minutes before it fell apart because of the thumping movement of the engines.

HMS Alecto

13

Amazing!
The steamship *Great Eastern* had three types of power – sails, paddle wheels and a propeller. It was built by Isambard Kingdom Brunel and launched in 1858. At the time it was the largest ship in the world.

Which steamers used paddles?

Before propellers were invented, most steamships used paddles driven by steam engines. Paddle steamers on the Mississippi River, USA, have one large stern paddle which works very well in shallow water.

Mississippi paddle steamer

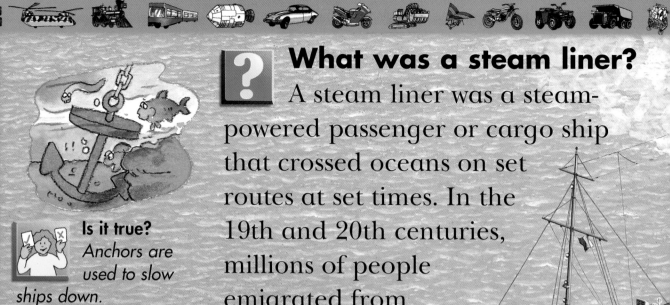

What was a steam liner?

A steam liner was a steam-powered passenger or cargo ship that crossed oceans on set routes at set times. In the 19th and 20th centuries, millions of people emigrated from Europe to America on steam liners, taking their own food and bedding.

Is it true? Anchors are used to slow ships down.

No. Anchors stop ships from floating away with the wind or tide. Anchors catch in rocks or sand on the seabed.

14

Amazing! Modern cruise liners are like huge floating hotels. There are cabins for thousands of passengers, restaurants, cinemas, theaters and lots of swimming pools.

Which modern liner has sails?

The luxury cruise liner *Club Med* has sails as well as an engine. Using the sails when the wind blows saves fuel for the engine.

Club Med 1

RMS Queen Mary (launched 1934)

Tug

15

? What does a tug do?

A tug is a boat with very powerful engines that pulls or pushes large ships. Tugs help to move ships in and out of port. They also go to the rescue of broken-down ships, and tow them back to port to be repaired.

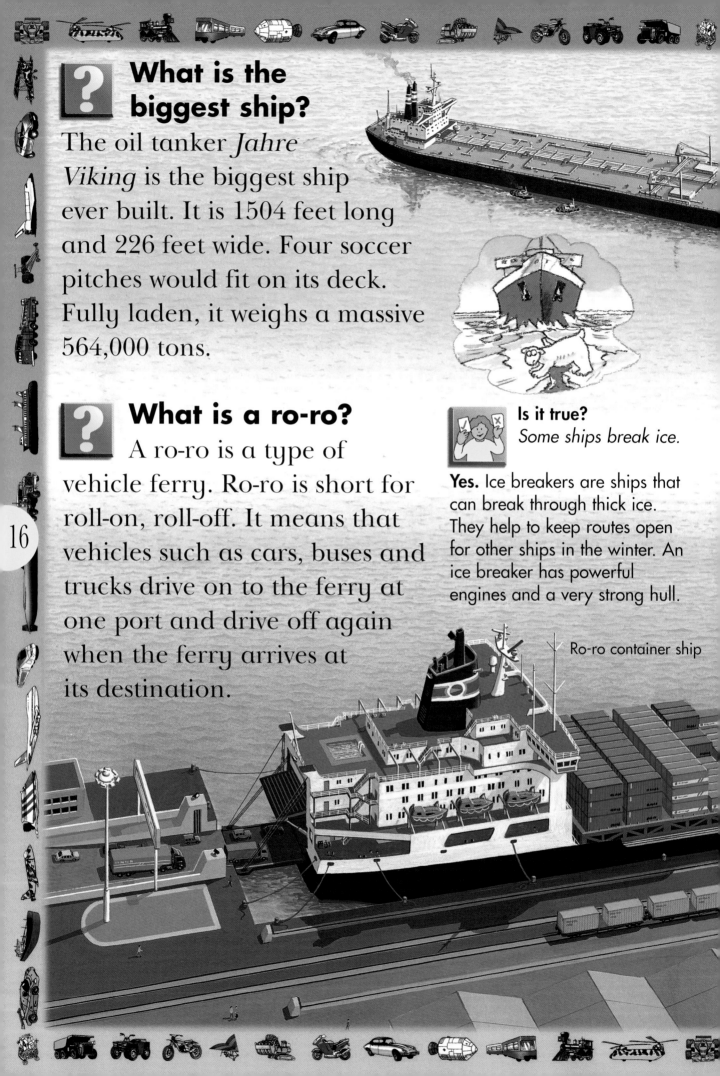

? What is the biggest ship?

The oil tanker *Jahre Viking* is the biggest ship ever built. It is 1504 feet long and 226 feet wide. Four soccer pitches would fit on its deck. Fully laden, it weighs a massive 564,000 tons.

? What is a ro-ro?

A ro-ro is a type of vehicle ferry. Ro-ro is short for roll-on, roll-off. It means that vehicles such as cars, buses and trucks drive on to the ferry at one port and drive off again when the ferry arrives at its destination.

Is it true?
Some ships break ice.

Yes. Ice breakers are ships that can break through thick ice. They help to keep routes open for other ships in the winter. An ice breaker has powerful engines and a very strong hull.

Ro-ro container ship

16

Jahre Viking oil tanker

Amazing! Some ships sink on purpose to rescue other ships. A semi-submersible ship sinks slowly down until its deck is under the water's surface. Then it moves beneath another ship and rises again to push the other ship up.

What is a container ship?

A container ship is a cargo ship that carries metal boxes called containers. The containers are piled on its deck and sometimes in its hold, too. Each container carries a different sort of cargo.

17

? Which boat has wings?

A hydrofoil has wings called foils. When a hydrofoil stops, its hull sits in the water. As the hydrofoil speeds up, its foils work like airplane wings and lift the hull out of the water. This makes it much easier for the hydrofoil to travel at high speed.

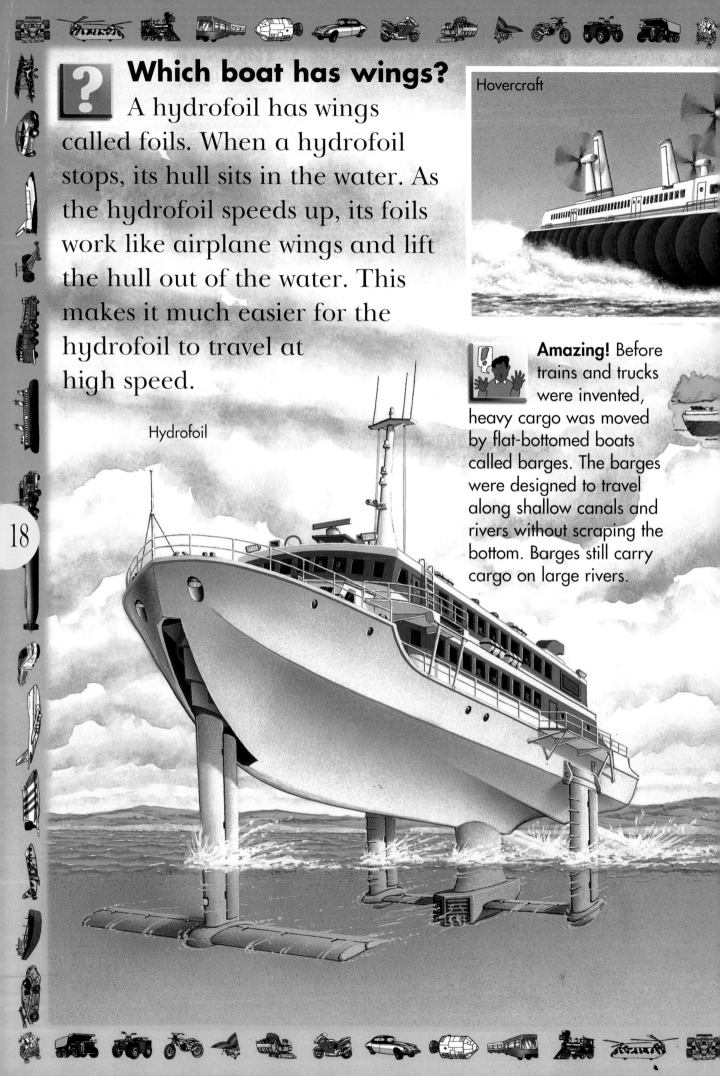

Hovercraft

Hydrofoil

Amazing! Before trains and trucks were invented, heavy cargo was moved by flat-bottomed boats called barges. The barges were designed to travel along shallow canals and rivers without scraping the bottom. Barges still carry cargo on large rivers.

Which boat flies?

A hovercraft is a boat which skims just above the water on a cushion of air. Huge fans blow air under the hovercraft. A rubber skirt holds the air in place. The hovercraft is moved along by propellers.

Which ship has two hulls?

A ship or boat with two hulls is called a catamaran. Catamarans can travel more quickly than ships with one hull which are called monohulls. High-speed ferries such as the SeaCat are catamarans. They have a top speed of more than 40 knots.

Is it true?
Some ships have three hulls.

Yes. A ship with three hulls is called a trimaran. Most trimarans are sailing yachts. They have a large hull in the center and two small side hulls. When one small hull is in the water, the other is in the air.

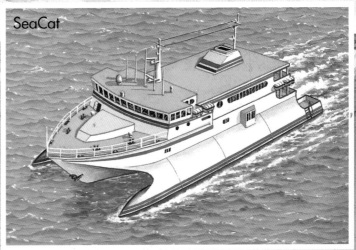
SeaCat

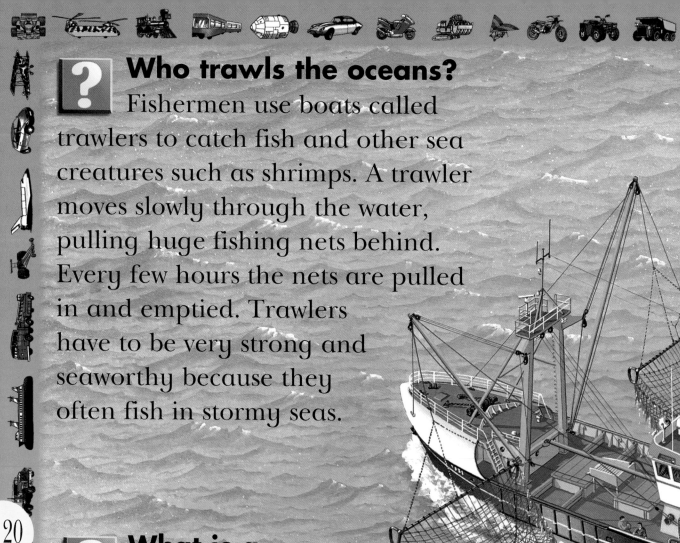

? Who trawls the oceans?

Fishermen use boats called trawlers to catch fish and other sea creatures such as shrimps. A trawler moves slowly through the water, pulling huge fishing nets behind. Every few hours the nets are pulled in and emptied. Trawlers have to be very strong and seaworthy because they often fish in stormy seas.

? What is a factory ship?

A factory ship is a huge fishing ship where fish are prepared for market. The catch can even be frozen and stored on board. Factory ships sometimes catch their own fish, but normally they store fish caught by a whole fleet of much smaller fishing boats.

Factory ship

Whaling ship

Shrimp trawler

❓ Who hunted whales?

Whalers were men who hunted whales for the oil in their blubber and also for their meat. When a whale was spotted, the whalers went after it in small boats and threw or fired spears, called harpoons, to kill it.

Amazing! Fishing boats called long liners catch fish on a fishing line up to 30 miles long. Hooks with bait are attached all the way along the line. Floats on the line have beacons that show where the line is in the dark.

Is it true?
People go fishing in kayaks.

Yes. Kayak is the proper name for a canoe with a deck on top and a small cockpit where the paddler sits. In the Arctic, Inuit fishermen hunt in kayaks made from wooden frames covered in seal skin.

❓ Which boats are unsinkable?

Lifeboats are rescue boats that don't sink even if they capsize (turn upside down). A lifeboat has a watertight cabin that makes it bob back upright. It has a strong hull and powerful engines for traveling quickly through rough seas.

Lifeboat

52-24

Amazing! The famous passenger liner *Titanic* was supposed to be unsinkable. But it sank on its maiden (first) voyage after hitting an iceberg in the North Atlantic Ocean in 1912.

Lightship

❓ What is a lightship?

A lightship is a ship with a lighthouse on its deck. Lightships are anchored near shallow water or dangerous rocks to warn sailors to keep clear. Most lightships have no crew because they are controlled automatically from shore.

Fire-fighting tug

Is it true?
Life savers row through surf to rescue people.

Yes. Lifeguards row boats designed to break easily through surf near the beach. When they're off duty, lifeguards also race their boats.

❓ Which boat puts out fires?

Fire-fighting tugs are like fire trucks at sea. They're designed to put out fires on ships, oil rigs, or in buildings on shore. They have powerful pumps which pump water from the sea to spray at fires.

23

Which ship is a floating airport?

An aircraft carrier has a huge, empty flat deck where aircraft take off and land. The aircraft take off from the bow using a catapult. They land again from the stern. Hooks on the planes catch a wire on deck, and stop the planes with a jolt. Underneath the deck are hangars where the aircraft are stored and serviced.

Amazing! The first gun battle between two ironclads (warships with iron armor) took place in 1862 during the American Civil War. The *Monitor* and the *Merrimack* fired at each other but no great damage was done.

American aircraft carrier

? What was a pocket battleship?

Pocket battleships were small, fast, German ships in the 1930s. Only three of them were built. Each had six huge guns, armor more than two inches thick and powerful diesel engines.

Is it true?
Some ships are nuclear-powered.

Yes. Some large submarines, some aircraft carriers and some ice breakers have nuclear-powered engines. They can travel for several months without having to re-fuel.

Admiral Graf Spee pocket battleship

25

? Which ship is invisible?

The United States Navy "stealth" warship doesn't show up clearly on enemy radar. Like the stealth aircraft, its special shape and paint scatter enemy radar signals making it very difficult to detect.

Stealth warship

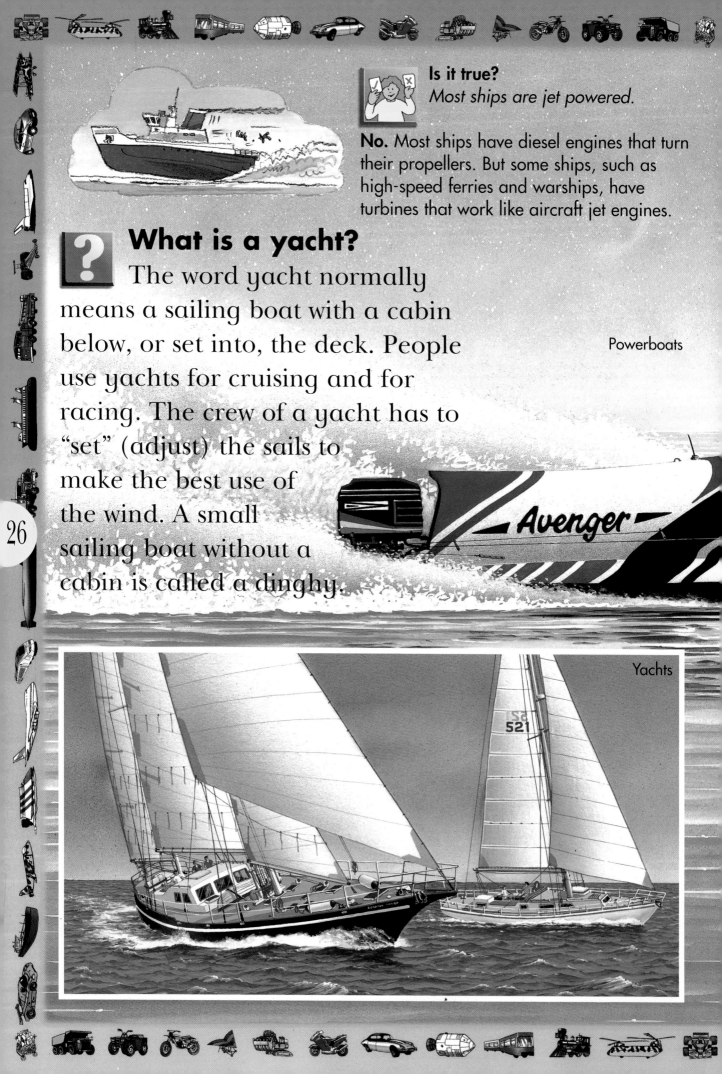

? What is a yacht?

The word yacht normally means a sailing boat with a cabin below, or set into, the deck. People use yachts for cruising and for racing. The crew of a yacht has to "set" (adjust) the sails to make the best use of the wind. A small sailing boat without a cabin is called a dinghy.

Powerboats

Avenger

26

Yachts

521

? Which boats can travel the fastest?

The fastest boats are powerboats, with top speeds of about 120 knots (138 mph). Most powerboats are used for racing. They have huge outboard engines at the back and skim across the water's surface, bouncing against the waves and any trapped air beneath them.

Amazing! Some boats are pushed along by water jets. A powerful pump sucks in water from under the boat and squirts it out of the back. This shoots the boat forwards. Jet-skis also use water jets.

JANNINE 31

25

27

Surfer

? Who surfs across waves?

Surfers ride down the sloping faces of waves balanced on their boards. Expert surfers can stay on a wave all the way to shore. They often ride through the "tube" formed by the curling top of the wave.

❓ How big are submarines?

The biggest submarines are nuclear-powered naval submarines. The biggest of all are Russian Typhoon submarines. They're 558 feet long (as long as two soccer pitches) and weigh about 26,500 tons. They can stay under water for months on end and sail around the world without refueling.

World War Two U-boat

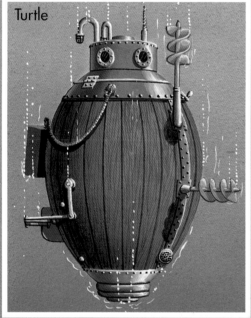

Turtle

❓ What was a U-boat?

U-boats were German submarines used in World War One and World War Two. U-boat is short for underwater boat. U-boats sank thousands of ships. They crept up silently, hidden under the water, and fired missiles called torpedoes. The torpedoes zoomed through the water and exploded when they hit the ships.

 **Amazing!** The first working submarine looked like a wooden barrel. It was built in 1776 and was called *Turtle*. The operator sat inside and pedaled to make its propellers turn. *Turtle* was designed to attack ships by diving under them and fixing a bomb to their hulls. But it was never successful.

Is it true?
*Submarines use
sound to see.*

Yes. A submarine's sonar
machine makes beeps of sound that spread out through
the water. If the sound hits an object in the water, it
bounces back to the submarine and is picked up by the
sonar machine. The machine works out how big the
object is and how far away it is.

29

Operating the periscope

❓ What is a periscope?

Submarine crews use their
periscopes to see ships on
the surface above them
when submarines are
submerged. The top of the
periscope sticks just above
the surface. It works using
several lenses and prisms
(triangular pieces of glass).

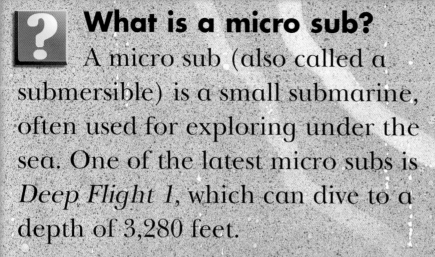

What is a micro sub?

A micro sub (also called a submersible) is a small submarine, often used for exploring under the sea. One of the latest micro subs is *Deep Flight 1*, which can dive to a depth of 3,280 feet.

Micro sub

Amazing! Divers who repair undersea pipelines and oil rigs wear strong diving suits, like mini submersibles. They can dive to about 1,000 feet. The divers have to breathe oxygen mixed with helium, which gives them very squeaky voices!

Is it true?
Submarines can dive to the bottom of the ocean.

No. The deepest a normal submarine can dive is about 2,300 feet. If a submarine went any deeper the huge water pressure would crush its hull and water would flood in.

Jason Junior

30

   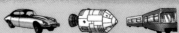

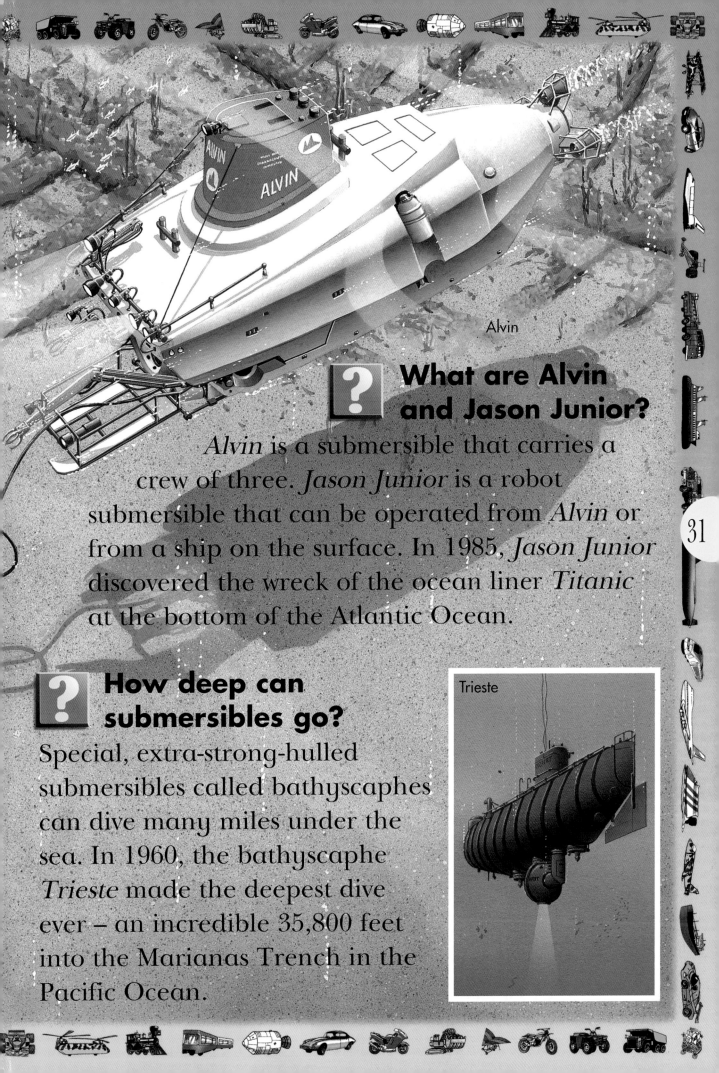

Alvin

? What are Alvin and Jason Junior?

Alvin is a submersible that carries a crew of three. *Jason Junior* is a robot submersible that can be operated from *Alvin* or from a ship on the surface. In 1985, *Jason Junior* discovered the wreck of the ocean liner *Titanic* at the bottom of the Atlantic Ocean.

? How deep can submersibles go?

Special, extra-strong-hulled submersibles called bathyscaphes can dive many miles under the sea. In 1960, the bathyscaphe *Trieste* made the deepest dive ever – an incredible 35,800 feet into the Marianas Trench in the Pacific Ocean.

Trieste

Glossary

Blubber A thick layer of warming fat under the skin of a whale or other sea mammal.

Bow The front part of a ship. It is normally pointed to break easily through the water.

Container A metal box on a ship, truck or train which can be filled with cargo.

Diesel engine A type of internal combustion engine that uses diesel oil as fuel.

Dug-out A type of canoe made by hollowing out a large tree trunk.

Hull The main part of ship or boat. It keeps the boat watertight and supports the decks.

Knot A measure of speed at sea. One knot is equal to one nautical mile (1.15 miles) per hour.

Paddle wheel A wheel with flat blades around the outside. The bottom of the wheel sits in the water. As a ship's paddle wheel turns, the paddles push the ship along.

Propeller A set of blades. When a ship's propeller spins round in the water, it pushes the ship along.

Rudder A flap at the stern of a ship or boat that turns from side to side to make the ship or boat turn left or right.

Stern The back part of a ship.

Tar A black, sticky, waterproof substance that goes runny when it is heated up and hardens again when it cools.

Torpedo An underwater missile that explodes when it hits a ship.

32

Index